Garden of Eve

poems by

Joanne Grumet

Finishing Line Press
Georgetown, Kentucky

Garden of Eve

Copyright © 2020 by Joanne Grumet
ISBN 978-1-64662-289-4 First Edition
All rights reserved under International and Pan-American Copyright Conventions. No part of this book may be reproduced in any manner whatsoever without written permission from the publisher, except in the case of brief quotations embodied in critical articles and reviews.

ACKNOWLEDGMENTS

"A Farmer's Kitchen," "Ars Poetica," "Happiness," "Journey of Discovery," "Tulips," and "Vivian's Pot" appeared in *BigCityLit.com*, as did an earlier version of "Alzheimer's."
"Ceremony at Jamaica Bay" and "Cutchogue" appeared in *Poetry Quarterly*.
"The Bath" and "Florida" appeared in *Jewish Women's Literary Annual*.
"Up at the Old Motel" appeared in *The Same*.

Publisher: Leah Maines
Editor: Christen Kincaid
Cover Art: Carin Kulb Dangot, www.carinkulbdangot.com
Author Photo: Lenny Bass, http://www.lennybass.com
Cover Design: Elizabeth Maines McCleavy

Order online: www.finishinglinepress.com
also available on amazon.com

Author inquiries and mail orders:
Finishing Line Press
P. O. Box 1626
Georgetown, Kentucky 40324
U. S. A.

Table of Contents

I. Garden of Eve

In the beginning 1

Pokeweed 2

Happiness 3

Alzheimer's 4

Wild Lupine 5

II. Passing Through

passing through 9

Ceremony at Jamaica Bay 10

Journey of Discovery 11

III. Beyond the Garden Wall

Ars Poetica 15

Up at the Old Motel 16

Tulips 17

Vivian's Pot 18

A Farmer's Kitchen 19

IV. Eve's Legacy

The Bath 23

Cutchogue 25

Florida 26

Daughter 27

This book is dedicated to my late husband, Scotty, who always said to me, "Go for it!"

I. Garden of Eve

In the beginning

sweet ripe rose hips
stained our fingertips
and lips orange. Hungry horseflies
harassed our flesh.

That long critter never lied to me
nor did I deceive my man
not in that garden,
not on this land.

Pokeweed

On a long stem
of small blooms
I grew, in Momma's
fragrant arms.

Hard green berry,
I lived the summer
through, indifferent to
her sweet florets as

they fell. In autumn,
songbirds came
for my deep-ripe fruit

and I learned to sing
the love she lavished
on me
that summer through.

Happiness

A small lizard lets me watch him
 up close. Sunning himself

on the porch, his chest pulses
his needle-fine nails hold on

He moves when I turn away
and then you are gone

and then you are gone

Alzheimer's

When darkness reached from under the pine
and the path was hidden away in fright
I lost my footing in tangled vines

The grass that June was perfumed with thyme
but something that day was not quite right
and darkness reached from under the pine

Slowing his steps he sat for a time
and when I saw him in his plight
I lost my footing in tangled vines

Nothing to do but stop our climb
as the frogs jumped away in fright
and darkness reached from under the pine

In the forest of grief I missed the signs
how to manage in day-turned-to-night
and I lost my footing in tangled vines

When the moan of the mourning dove combined
with the flap of her wings in frenzied flight
when darkness reached from under the pine
I lost my footing in tangled vines

Wild Lupine

Where land has been torn up
and there is emptiness
wild lupine grows

after a great love goes

Where butterflies feed
and flutter all day
and tall spikes of purple sway

pain no longer shows

II. Passing Through

passing through

i.
the buzz of a fly
tears a hole in the silence
and the universe

ii.
our silver grey cat
mysteriously as mist
slips back to this world

Ceremony at Jamaica Bay

Upon release the terrapin,
bold patterns on his back, flails
about for traction
in the sand

Does he understand the Buddhists' prayer
for his safety in this life,
higher consciousness
in the next?

Or does he only hear the drone
of the weed-whacker
as it trims the edges
of the path?

Journey of Discovery

The train heads west into the coal-filled hills
of West Virginia.
We stop amid the bogs; the stumps of birch
white above the water.

This is no ordinary train, no Amtrak,
no Pennsylvania Railroad;
this is a dream train back to childhood
on the banks of the Ohio.

The conductor is an old woman
with long white braids.
She spreads herself out on a grassy hill,
opening to the music of this place.

I climb down the slick black rocks
carefully. My body listens
for where to place my feet,
how to stick to stone.

Then it's up again and
with each step an incantation
against the dangers of the pit:
dirty—dark—dank—

Almost at the top, one last step,
and I need another "d";
I smile as it comes:
democracy—

and an eagle emerges from the stone
to my rescue.

I'm on the train now
heading back East.
Or am I the train?

The porters are busy
taking down the doors
between the cars.
No more first and second class riders,
it is announced.

I discover I am free
and equal
in all my parts,
all of me.

III. Beyond the Garden Wall

Ars Poetica

It's great to wake up
on a mountain top
after a steep climb
and still have time
to dream

Down below
I watch myself
pick up dollar bills
scattered on city streets
like dead leaves

but up here
I witness
the birth of clouds
as lacy mists rise
from creek beds
into morning
into breath

In a nearby village
hidden away
beside a white church
on a lane swept back
around the mountain's curve
stands a house of poetry

I turn a phrase inside out
like a pulled off sweater
and wipe my feet on the mat
as I enter

Up at the Old Motel

The mountain town is past its prime
but survives; raspberries ramble
along the road, the valley is still wide.

Weeds crack the blacktop in the lot
where I'm waiting for the maid:
she's lean, a smoker, worn.

I swat mosquitoes and tell her
the lock on the porch door's broken;
also, the window screen is torn.

She never looks at me

so I am guarded, too
but wonder if she knows
the people I once knew.

The new resort above the town
looks down on us but fuck them,
they don't have this mountain view.

Tulips

I love to buy them closed
tight as dancers' thighs
and watch them leap open
in my warm room

Their colorful skirts balloon
and slowly, slowly they lower
over their green-leafed base
and dry in place as if posed

Let me die, too, after
such a show

Vivian's Pot

> *Meanwhile the slap and thump of palm and thumb*
> *On wet mis-shapenness begins to hum*
> —John Hollander, "The Mad Potter"

Eros we understand
with our fingers, our palms,
as when we touch
a lover's silky arms
but Apollo demands
decorum of art:
you must not touch.

A potter even so enjoys
wet mud so much
when as midwife she
slaps the clay to life.

And thereby came into creation
a tall ceramic vase
whose glazed lip chipped
while in my possession,
but whose integrity remains intact.

What pleasure to get flowers
the right length and fullness
for this vase, what pleasure later,
while putting the piece away,
to trace where the potter's hands
have smoothed the porous slab of clay.

A Farmer's Kitchen

(Photograph by Walker Evans)

a bare room
in Alabama

an old towel
hanging on a peg
so neatly

wood table,
chair,

a water jug

hard times.

IV. Eve's Legacy

The Bath

It was July
on a lawn
on a high cliff
above the Sound
in Cutchogue.

Only the gulls and osprey,
blackbirds and catbirds
could see us
as we took the sun.

No hot water in the house,
no indoor tub,
Cousin Joycie and I

and Aunt Fran
pulled the tin washtub
from under the beach-house
and filled it from a hose.

Water splashed
onto the hot flagstones,
onto warm grass
as Joycie and I bathed
our skinny young
bodies.

Then Aunt Fran
took her turn in the tub

her body white, soft,
voluptuous
her grey hair piled high
on her head
her bush still henna red.

She washed
and dried herself
modestly and with
great pleasure.

Mother stood by
laughing
with her Brownie camera
and posed us
in a graceful
drapery
of towels.

Cutchogue

Aunt Fran's cherry cordial
sits on a shelf away
from bright summer light

The cherry tree is long gone
cut down by storms
and then the saw.

The lilac is gone as well, where
Fran and Jack were buried
on the cliff,

the wind hollowing out
their place of rest,
setting their ashes adrift.

But memories of summer
persist like wild honeysuckle
on the hill

and for now the cordial
keeps, red and thick
and sweet.

Florida

Troops of landscapers
slight and wiry
in their Day-Glow vests
fight back the looming growth
of scrubland.

They edge walkways of fancy residences,
trim hedges, harvest the fallen leaves
from messy palms.

I recognize these young men as recent arrivals
to these swamplands
where melaleuca and pepper berry trees
have joined the native flora
and thrived,
although not always welcome.

They are more exposed to the sun
than transplants from the North:
the Canadians, Vermonters and New Yorkers
who survive inside, in air-conditioned niches.

I do not know them, have only smiled hello,
but they remind me of the slender youths
who dug my mother's grave down here
in the sandy soil.

I wanted so much to speak with them—
her final caretakers—
as they waited quietly for the last mourner,
a lingering daughter,
to leave them to their work.

Daughter

Watching your children grow
has brought you pleasure and stabbing
pain, anger at me old and new
and very real

Today we walk in the woods,
examining a boulder
evenly carved into layers by
nature's hand

I show you a white violet
tinged with purple, you catch
a tiny tree toad
for the young ones' delight

and point out to me
the wondrous patterns on a fern:
its deeply scalloped edges,
deeply scalloped.

Joanne Grumet was born in New York City and got her degrees in Linguistics from Queens College, the University of Michigan at Ann Arbor, and New York University. She was a lexicographer and worked on dictionaries for Funk and Wagnall's and Random House. She taught Linguistics at New York University and Montclair State University and Writing at the City University of New York. Her poems have been published in *The Poetry Quarterly, The Same*, and *Jewish Women's Literary Annual*, as well as online at *BigCityLit.com*. In addition, her poetry is in the archives of the Brooklyn Museum. Joanne also writes songs, and she and her music and poetry have been featured on the cable TV show *The Song*, out of Deerfield, Massachusetts. Her songs can be heard at *www.reverbnation.com/summerwind*

www.ingramcontent.com/pod-product-compliance
Lightning Source LLC
LaVergne TN
LVHW041506070426
835507LV00012B/1372